THE
WHITE
WAVE

1983

Agnes Lynch Starrett

Poetry Prize

The
White
Wave

Kate
Daniels

Kate Daniell (signature)

University of Pittsburgh Press

Published by the University of Pittsburgh Press, Pittsburgh, Pa. 15260
Copyright © 1984, Kate Daniels
All rights reserved
Feffer and Simons, Inc., London
Manufactured in the United States of America
Second printing 1986

Library of Congress Cataloging in Publication Data

Daniels, Kate, 1953–
  The white wave.

  (Pitt poetry series)
  I. Title. II. Series.
PS3554.A5636W45 1984   811'.54   83-40341
ISBN 0-8229-3493-0
ISBN 0-8229-5359-5 (pbk.)

Some of these poems have originally appeared in the following publications: *Crazyhorse* ("Christmas Party," "Elegy," "For Miklos Radnóti: 1909–1944," and "Grandmother, I'm Reading Tolstoy"); *IRIS* ("Small But Strong"); *Ironwood* ("My Father's Desk" and "The Smallest Movement"); *Massachusetts Review* ("On the River"); *New England Review* ("Sometimes When I'm Singing"); *Pequod* ("What Will Happen"); *Plainsong* ("Hundertwasser and the Six-Year-Olds" and "The Playhouse"); *Poetry Now* ("Pyracantha"); *Skyline* ("Alcestis"); and *Virginia Quarterly Review* ("Epilogue: After a Murder").

"My Father's Desk" received a Pushcart Prize for 1982 and was reprinted in *The Pushcart Anthology: Best of the Small Presses VII* (New York: The Pushcart Press, 1982).

"Sometimes When I'm Singing" also appeared in the *1984 Anthology of Magazine Verse and Yearbook of American Poetry* (Beverly Hills: Monitor Book Company, 1984).

"Christmas Party," "Elegy," "For Miklos Radnóti: 1909–1944," and "Grandmother, I'm Reading Tolstoy" received the 1983 *Crazyhorse* Poetry Award.

The epigraph on page 29 is taken from "The Inquiry," in *The Collected Poems of Weldon Kees* (Lincoln: University of Nebraska Press, 1975).

I would like to extend my particular thanks to Mark Rudman and David Wojahn for their help in preparing this book for publication.

*The publication of this book is supported by grants
from the National Endowment for the Arts
in Washington, D.C., a Federal agency,
and the Pennsylvania Council on the Arts.*

for Richard Jones

CONTENTS

Family Gathering   ix

I. Bodies of Kin

My Father's Desk   3
Sometimes When I'm Singing   5
Portrait with Money   7
Self-Portrait with Politics   8
Why I Don't Write You Anymore   11
The Playhouse   13
Pyracantha   14
Alcestis   15
Small But Strong   16
Hundertwasser and the Six-Year-Olds   17
Winter Coats   19
The Smallest Movement   21

II. The White Wave

On the River   25
Epilogue: After a Murder   26
Tribulations   28
After the Operation   29
What Will Happen   31
For Miklos Radnóti: 1909–1944   33
Christmas Party   36
Grandmother, I'm Reading Tolstoy   38
Apologia   39
Rushing Away   40
Geese in Snow   41
Why We Won't   42
Elegy   43
Not Singing   44

FAMILY GATHERING
1959

The long sweat over the sink after the huge meal.
The women—aunts, mothers, grown cousins, grandmothers—
trading places in the assembly line of scrape and wash, wipe and
  dry.
Slow and calm. Their full cotton skirts twirling under their knees,
their hair kinked up and sprayed in place.
In some ignored corner, I undress an unconvincing plastic doll
or run my fingers over the pictures in a book and watch them
pass the dishes back and forth, the thin white cups, the vacant
  smiles
of expensive plates. Back and forth, they see each other in each
  other's
faces, materialize the reasons they've gathered again—
no holiday season, no special occasion—to stand and wash
at this double mouth of sink, to count each other and think
how old everyone else has gotten, to test the links. Now the meal
  is over,
the men puffing and burping on the screened side porch.
From my solitary corner, I study the men and watch
my oldest cousin Jonathan unclank his belt and lean
back sighing, and remember *Jonathan and me on a raft*
in the ocean two or three summers gone when I fell off and sunk
in gray water under gray sky of laundry suds and scum
when there was no floor no sand and I was not scared
for once looking around under the crashing waves
for once I was not scared and then there was a hand
Jonathan's hand with its gold and ruby ring
finding me in the surliness of ocean and hurting me and hurling
  me
up through the noisy water to the common rubber raft.

All the men are smoking and picking their teeth
with cardboard matchbook covers and flipping ashes on the floor
and spreading thighs wide on the plastic furniture, making
crinkling sounds on the slick cushions and farting and
burping and pulling smoke in and out of their slightly opened
    mouths.
And the women, the women moving soft in the next room with
    the sounds
I love, sounds like butter, and the crisp sound the coffee can
    makes
when it first gets punctured. Sounds like grass, growing
when you listen close, ear on earth, deliciously silent
screams and moans you pretend you hear. The refrigerator
    swooshes
shut and buzzes like a heart. A high heel clicks
on linoleum. Someone is folding a sodden linen towel
and someone else is holding her hands up to the light
that falls in through the checkered curtain
and bathing them in lotion to make them soft
again. Now she is slipping on her rings and turning
up the stones to face the world.
Inside, against the fatty pad of finger flesh,
in the time and sweat-worn silver band,
two names connected with an ampersand, and a date
twelve years from where I hover in my corner
studying the married women's placid faces and smooth hair,
remembering *the strong sounds in the bedroom the night*
I walked out of a bad dream of red water and wind
dream shaking my canopied bed like a boat   walked into theirs
and heard the sounds of animal   not family   not
Mother with the pincurls in her hair

x

her cold feet and furry slippers   not Father
in the suit   the late nights at work   the worn
billfold and the odor of tobacco.
The newest one is crying again and someone
must bring a breast for him to suck, someone
must smooth his head and cluck over him and wipe
his tiny penis dry and make him clean again.
There is noise when he sucks. There is air gasping
and infant moans deep in the throat and tiny fingers
opening and closing and the eagerness and the hunger
and the mother being sucked.
The mother rocking in the blue chair, the low lullaby
of cow and her hair a brown mirror of mine.
Now I'm thinking of the journey of the roast beef and gravy,
the coconut cake, the potato salad with little chips of pickle
and ham, all this sameness descending through bodies of kin
and turning different—blue and green and brown eyes,
four hair colors, crying babies and silent babies,
the short and the tall, the very pretty, the plum ugly.
The food going down and doing its whimsical dance and doing
different and talking in gurgles in all the stomachs
and doing its dance. Outside the other little ones
shriek and socialize and scream while they can, get dirty
while they can and touch each other everywhere while they can.
Undifferentiated bodies and voices and no urges are all urges
and the world is not a mouth it's a food.
I sit in the corner and run my fingers over the pictures
in the books and follow the symbols and signs
on the flat page and try to make them fat. Feel different
in my plaid skirt, my tortoise-shell barrette
that makes me look like all the others but funny things inside my
    head.

I close my eyes and feel moving, feel physics proving
right, proving it's spaces not solids, spaces and movement
inside the lines of things. Now the men are getting up and
    moving
inside as the sun goes under and the world shudders
in a chill. The dishes are dripping in the red drainer.
The men are hitching their trousers and coughing and sucking
one last smoke. Casting their eyes around uneasily, pretending
    not to see
the empty places on the lawn where the tree shadows yawn
and tell them to come on anyway. In a back room, the women
are smoothing sewing patterns on a bedspread
and tickling the baby with milk on its chin and counting
the children through the bedroom window and calling them in.
And I am in my corner feeling it move under me like a body,
    slow and strong.
Not fast: flowing and torpid. Not weak: wide and clenching,
stretching to fit the long moment.
My hair is brown.
My father's hair is brown.
My brother's hair is brown.
The baby's hair will soon be brown.
I see my mother's fingers in my fingers
twirling the bride doll in my lap. My fingers
busy under the covers under the ruffled canopy
what it feels like hairy down there and soft-smelling.
What it means.
My uncle's hard laugh, his glasses glinting crazily
in the first lit lamp. The scarred knees of his only son.
My glasses hooked over my ears, making everything bigger.
My grandmother's soft bun of brown hair
going gray. And the baby holding the deep hem
of her dress and pulling like I did,

at one, over the furnace's heated grid, falling
and burning crisscross nests of pinkish scars
on my lower legs. Now I cover them up. Now
I trace them with my finger. Now my father
still doesn't know how to touch me. He sees my scars
and puts his hand like a crown on top of my head
too roughly and it hurts. Then it's gone.
He's gone and the unintended roughness starts
soaking into the strange universe of movement around me,
into the dance that danced me so impossibly here
from these strangers' tall and barricaded bodies
to my own small collection of flesh and bone.

I

Bodies of Kin

Progress is not the aim, but circulation.
—Robert Frost

MY FATHER'S DESK

The wrinkles in the taxi driver's face—
I want to lie down there
and make them smooth again.
He might be fifty, my father's age,
everything about him public and accounted for.
He can't hide anything.
I thought I knew my father
because I recognized his big, red ears,
the way he eats his corn.
But this might be my father
and I, someone else, looking at him.

It's hard to care about the rich girl
who weakens after seeing an old man on Broadway
killed by a car.
She said his cane lay there
like an exclamation mark.
She said the day was so perfect—then this!
She wanted me to make her tea.
I wanted to see the dead man
lying in the wet, black street
and know the place he came from,
where he was going: a chilled flat,
rice boiling on the stove.
He just stepped out to buy a paper.
The dog yaps at the door
awaiting his return
but he never comes back.
The yellow carpet is just the shade

of the one in my father's office,
worn under the desk where he shuffles his feet.
Like the old man, he wants to get up and stroll
out into the rain to buy a pack of cigarettes
or just to look at the waitress with the big, soft rear.

Thirty years at the same desk.
I've never looked inside
to find what he might have hidden there:
the funny pack of sugar, a picture
the secretary snapped of him where—
caught in the brief, kind light—
he looks famous! The dark spot
on top where he rests his head.
The secret note he wrote himself,
"I am fifty now. 50."

The cabbie's voice is loud and tired.
He's just another person with a crummy job.
My father was another lousy father.
But now I can forgive him that.
I know the way it feels
to stay awake and work when all you want
is to lay your head in someone's lap and sleep.

I remember the way he touched me as a child,
the delicate latch of his fingers
on my weakling arm. I was so fresh
he was afraid for me—afraid I would break.
Something the world could never feel for me.

SOMETIMES WHEN I'M SINGING

Somewhere someone is listening to me.
A widower twiddling the dials
of his cabinet radio
or a young boy laid up in bed
all summer with a broken leg.
Outside, the dark filters down
like salt and pepper. He can hear
the shouts of his friends
leaping the creek that borders the ball field
but all he can do is think
or scratch out the rhythm of a song
that bothers him on his heavy cast.

There's a woman who walks with her hand
on the pain where her breast was.
I am the song in her head
that tells her, *go on.*
She can hear me all day
and at night in bed
the acknowledging, full ache
of loss can't play as loud as me.
Because I know the way she feels
about her husband sleeping in another room.
She wants him back.

The five-year-old who died
yesterday never woke up
after the stupid accident.
Her parents didn't know how to make it easy

for her. But I was there. I helped her
over the white wave that was soft and gentle
because she was little.
In the end, the parents heard me, too.
The smile I made her leave behind
made them still. They put out
their hands to touch it
as if it were a flower
they could keep
if only they took it
fast enough
before the edges withered
in the stinging air.

PORTRAIT WITH MONEY

At the end of the day, my father is tired.
He sighs over his newspaper and pushes
the cold dinner around on his plate.
Because he works late, he eats alone.
Even my mother will not sit with him.
She is tired, too, from her day at the office
and is folding clothes or making lunches
for tomorrow or is already asleep
in front of the chuckling television set.

As young as I am, I know about money:
How there is never enough, how it causes
crying and fights. On payday, I know
happiness again—a new pair
of saddle shoes, a movie after school,
the red plaid skirt on the beautiful girl
in the Sears catalogue, page three-sixty-two.

When my father goes to bed at night
he leaves his wallet on the hall table.
Most often, there is nothing in it
but a couple of ones or fives.
In the plastic window for photographs
there is a picture of him and me when I was one.
We look so happy together. I hold him
so tightly on the arm and neck
there's no space between us,
but he hasn't started to mind. Somehow,
small and fair and held so close, I can see
how I could look like a growth on him, something
permanent and needy, something he didn't ask for
but is learning to live with.

SELF-PORTRAIT WITH POLITICS

At the dinner table, my brother says something
Republican he knows I will hate.
He has said it only for me, hoping
I will rise to the argument as I usually do
so he can call me "communist"
and accuse me of terrible things—not loving
the family, hating the country, unsatisfied
with my life. I feel my fingers tighten
on my fork and ask for more creamed potatoes
to give me time to think.

He's right: It's true I am not satisfied
with life. Each time I come home
my brother hates me more for the life
of the mind I have chosen to live.
He works in a factory and can never understand
why I am paid a salary for teaching poetry
just as I can never understand his factory job
where everyone loves or hates the boss like god.
He was so intelligent as a child
his teachers were scared of him.
He did everything well and fast
and then shot rubberbands at the girls' legs
and metal lunchboxes lined up neatly beneath the desks.
Since then, something happened I don't know about.
Now he drives a forklift every day.
He moves things in boxes from one place
to another place. I have never worked
in a factory and can only imagine
the tedium, the thousand escapes
the bright mind must make.

But tonight I will not fight again.
I just nod and swallow and in spite
of everything remember my brother as a child.
When I was six and he was five, I taught him everything
I learned in school each day while we waited for dinner.
I remember his face—smiling always,
the round, brown eyes, and how his lower lip
seemed always wet and ready to kiss.
I remember for a long time his goal in life
was to be a dog, how we were forced
to scratch his head, the pathetic sound
of his human bark. Now he glowers
and acts like a tyrant and cannot eat
and thinks I think
I am superior to him.

The others ignore him as they usually do:
My mother with her bristly hair.
My father just wanting to get back to the TV.
My husband rolling his eyes in a warning at me.

It has taken a long time to get a politics
I can live with in a world that gave me
poetry and my brother an assembly line.
I accept my brother for what he is
and believe in the beauty of work
but also know the reality of waste,
the good minds ground down through circumstance
and loss. I mourn the loss of all I think
he could have been, and this is what he feels,
I guess, and cannot face and hates me

for reminding him of what is gone and wasted
and won't come back.

For once, it's too sad to know all this.
So I give my brother back his responsibility
or blandly blame it all on sociology,
and imagine sadly how it could have been different,
how it will be different for the son I'll bear.
And how I hope in thirty years he'll touch
his sister as they touched as children
and let nothing come between the blood they share.

WHY I DON'T WRITE YOU ANYMORE

Winter is coming on again.
That was always your favorite season.
The shrunken shrubs, the flower bulbs
drawn down into their winter tunnels,
the frozen ground—all remind me of you,
dormant and stunted till summer comes.

In winter, you kept me locked inside
with a high fire heating the furnace's metal grid.
Hot cocoa and coconut cookies, socks
miraculously turned into dolls,
the bear coat in the bedroom closet
—all conspired to make me forget
the world outside where I wanted to go.
And with no leaves on the trees
you had a clear view from the house
to the end of the yard:
Easy to see who was coming
and drive them away.

I learned the unpolluted, fanatical
sound of love from you:
It echoed long and loud
through the winter air around your house
like gunshots that keep coming
even after the animal is dead.

If I could come to you now I would
untie the tapes that tie you down at night.
You could tell me one more time
how you safety-pinned the blankets over me
in my wooden crib so I couldn't kick them off,

remind me of the dozen times each night
you checked my sleep, sacrificed your own
to count my breaths, feel my feet, watching
the light from the streetlamp play figures
on my face, foretell the person I would be.

If I could come to you now
I would hold your soft, historical hand
all night long and keep you safe
from winter, that ungrowing season
you always loved—it is all so soft, so slow,
how people freeze to death, you know—
now it has you in its mitt
and won't let go.

THE PLAYHOUSE

My dolls came alive in it,
all of them whining in unison.
And there was a pink curtain.
I'd part it and see your hand
flailing at the bedroom window,
beckoning me in.

But my dolls needed me, too,
wetting their little diapers,
mewing *Ma-Ma* whenever I thumped
their stomachs.
I pretended my hair was long
like yours, draped a black towel
over my head and nuzzled the dollies
till it fell over them
covering their faces.

Each of us in our houses:
I thought of you combing your hair
before the mirror,
chatting about men who had loved you,
how my father was a fool,
what you wished you had done.

I never knew why you wanted me.
I was alone out there. I loved you
away from the spectre of your black hair
gleaming in the mirror, your lovely face
talking to itself.

PYRACANTHA

Those bitter orange bullets
exploded every fall
next to the kitchen door.
You tended them on hands and knees
crushing one on your thumb
to show me the pulp and poison.

I chanted pyracantha, pyracantha,
and tied up bits with string
for your bedside table.
You loved its acridness,
the way it was nailed

into the nights he took you,
your cheek pressed in the pillow,
legs drawn up, pyracantha
oozing poison, your eyes drawn
to the tiny thorns of flame.

ALCESTIS

To escape him and my traitorous body
made me happy.
The nights he crept into my room
sucking himself to sleep,
great wings I could not beat down
rose in me.
He was only there for himself,
slept afterwards,
while I smoothed the feathers of my heart
afraid to grow frail and hysterical.
I wanted the company of cold people
who would never touch me.
Death, the little I saw of it,
was satisfying. Even if accidentally
they touched each other,
their fingers slid right through
leaving no print.
And their eyes were frozen balls
I could look into and not see myself.

Back here in my husband's house
I can't stop thinking about it—
the huge paw of Hercules
strangling my saviour,
how I tried running farther on
so I could never come back.
Blue veins beat on the hand
that ripped me back to life.
There was nothing cold about the fingers
that wrenched my shoulders
and left their marks,
singe marks of the fire
licking my body
I try and try to quench, but cannot.

15

SMALL BUT STRONG

An antique candlestick of tangerine-colored glass
has graced a table in my parents' house
since they were wed. Inherited, handed down
from wife to wife on my mother's side,
full of tiny chips and ancient nicks,
still the color floods out warm and true
whenever afternoon sun pours through.

At eight or nine, I saw my mother,
only five-two and very light,
lift it up in the middle of a fight
and throw her child-sized hand
behind her shoulder as if to strike
my father shouting down at her.

Perhaps he knew better than I
she would not hit him,
what devils raged in her freckled hand
with its modest rings. Maybe he,
familiar in the long, dark corridors
of married life, saw the candlestick for what it was—
unused, unlit—and recognized no need to raise his arm
so he would not be hit.

The way it slowly traveled down again
to the polished wooden top,
the tiny tremble of the colored glass
in the whitened, angry fist
became my first lesson in taking back,
reneging on the ugliness that lives in love
and makes us frantic to drive it out,
to light all the lamps and candles
in the house, pretending
all, for once, is well.

HUNDERTWASSER
AND THE SIX-YEAR-OLDS

I love Hundertwasser because so many people think his paintings look like they're done by children. "Even my six-year-old Joey could've done *that*," they cry, pointing to the framed Hundertwasser print on my mantle, the one called *The Miraculous Draft*. I love Hundertwasser because his joyous paintings with their brilliant blue backgrounds and tiny, fishlike people make me feel I'm in kindergarten again, when I wasn't afraid to make the world any way I wanted it to be. I painted tree trunks orange and purple, and the faces of mothers red or light blue in distress. I drew people taller than mountains and birthday cakes as large as swimming pools. I had a long, flat carton of crayons that thrilled me with its invitation to change the world.

In the Hundertwasser I have, the eight large gold birds are as important as the people. Their eyes are wide open and looking steadily in all directions. Each of them has one hidden eye looking into the canvas, and one eye looking out. Six brown people in funny hats, tourists, I think, are sitting in a gaily painted boat that is passing in front of a town. In real life, these people would be too big for the boat. They would sink, and the world would have another tragedy: "Six Drowned on Vacation" the headlines would say. There would be coffins and the bloated bodies and weeping relatives taking tranquilizers in the funeral home. But in Hundertwasser's painting, these six saved people glide along in their fancy boat waving and picking fish from the water and dangling their legs over the side in a lighthearted way. They're on vacation for all of us. They make us feel better about every person who ever drowned because deep in the water beneath their overcrowded boat lies a turquoise semicircle full of big-eyed fish. It might be something as common as a fishing net, the way a six-year-old would draw it. On the other hand, it might be an underwater railroad, the place drowned people go, out of the dangerous currents

17

and fear of depths, out of real life where people act their age and paint like photographs.

We all knew how the world *could* be when we were six and unleashed our powers on our fingerpaints and crayon boxes. What we didn't know was how it really was. So this is a poem for all the six-year-olds in Hundertwasser, the brave ones in the blue world who grew up and also refused to grow up, who are six and six hundred, who saw it all with one eye and painted it with the other.

WINTER COATS

It's best in rush hour on the subway
when everyone is so tired from typing or punching
the cash register all day, or delivering packages,
that they let their bodies sag a little
out of weariness. Everyone is touching
someone else, and we can smell each other's
winter coats, the details of a thousand lives
recorded in the stubborn fibers of wool and cotton and synthetic
    fur.
The lady next to me smells like mothballs and Vicks Vaporub.
The teenager across the aisle dozes in a cloud
of turtle oil and fresh wood shavings.
Suddenly, I have a circle of friends,
the large family I always wanted. I can go home
with all these people to their houses and apartments,
help them out of their overcoats and peacoats,
their leather jackets and fake fur coats.
I can lock the door behind them and remember
the first coat closet I ever knew: my mother's
ugly European boots far back in the corner stuffed with paper,
trying to forget the war and everything horrible
they had walked over and waded through.
My father's outdoor shoes stained with grass and burst open
at one toe where his chronic hangnail demanded space.
The old keys and coins adrift in the pockets
of our solemn-colored coats that remembered everything
about all the places we'd ever lived.

Here on the subway, without fear of being sentimental,
we can slap our hands against our arms
and have something to talk about.

We can say, "It's awfully cold today, isn't it?"
and share the smell of our homelife that's locked
into the fabric of our winter coats
with everyone on the subway that has its own peculiar odor
of people crowded together, just wanting to get home
fast to the pot roast or chalupas, race results
or evening news, everyone sharing the same need
to hang up their coats in the heated hall, warm at last, and home.

THE SMALLEST MOVEMENT

Sometimes in the park
a woman rests on a bench,
her legs spread wide as a sleeping child's.
You can see underneath her skirt
she is naked and worn-out.
Telling myself that place
is really a flower
is my method of making her go away.
She can sleep on the bench until snow covers her.
I can lie in bed with the white blanket
up to my neck, pretending I'm cold.

In the hospital, one man's cancer
was different: it grew straight up
from his bones and burst through his skin.
It was easy to call it *trees*
grown too close to a sidewalk.
His wife was pale and small, her grief simple
to imagine. Her bones were so thin
but she wanted to give them to him.
They were harmless.

There is nothing beautiful about the fly
crawling on the starving child's face.
The image enters. Locked deep inside,
it cannot be transformed.
But there is another picture:
everyone joining hands for a moment
though it's impossible to hold on.
Even the smallest movement—
someone's hand chasing a fly—
is enough to break the chain.

II

The White Wave

Say it, say that there is hope.
—Miklos Radnóti

ON THE RIVER

How I came to live here
is Buñuel's story of the peasants
who ravaged their landlord's mansion.
Wealth was suddenly theirs
but they were too clumsy with sadness
to use it.

All day I look out the window
at the sluggish roll of the river.
People pass by on their boats
forgetting they're human.
Their casual waves touch nothing in me.
They glide away easily
but the slap of their wake on the bulkhead
eats away at the stone.
I hear each little wave with clarity.
They are like hands being clapped for attention
as if I were a servant being called to my master.

EPILOGUE: AFTER A MURDER

Time is my enemy
and my saviour.
I have stopped thinking,
if only I had been there.
I have stopped imagining
a different scene.

In the cold black gates
of the place where it happened
Neptune swims on fiercely,
trapped in an iron ocean of time.
The bloodstains scrubbed away,
the body no more than a few atoms
anyone anywhere might inhale.

There is no ending
to stories of grief.
There is no closure.
Only the gradual
acclimation of the living
carved up into different people,
their hearts curtained off
into solitary shrines,
pictures of the loved one
hung on nails behind the eyes.

The trees of Central Park
pop up incongruously
from the black heart of the city.
Walking anywhere, I might find him
again: If I study my hand
hard enough, it becomes something else:
an instrument of love, not torture.

I laid the baby in his crib
and tucked the blankets round him
while he sobbed, "good-bye, good-bye"
for good night because he didn't want to sleep.

The soft curve of his forehead
fringed with yellow hair
is a bulwark to time—
the undeveloped brain,
the memory that won't keep
either pain or pleasure
in its tiny plot.
"Say good night," I said, not

good-bye, the word that never ends.
Its long *i* calling out
for the lost one forever
saying, I am scared without you,
I am lonely.
I am missing something
since your death.
Give it back.

TRIBULATIONS

Until it's over
each day unfolds un-
evenly, the way the hand-dipped
candle flames: first, the brief explosion
of the struck match and the tall bright
burning-down of wick.
Then long periods of steady flaming.
But every now and then the light stabs
upward into farther reaches of darkness
and shows the shape of something worse,
and hurts, flames violently
from a weak spot in the candle wax,
a hidden bubble where oxygen hides
like a dangerous predator in a forest cave.
It leaps out burning and hungry
to devour the inattentive, the weak.
Those worn down by sorrow and misery
who got on this path by mistake
and only want a little steady light
to make out what's left of their lives.

AFTER THE OPERATION

The streets are full of broken glass,
Sparkling in this frenzied noon.
With naked feet and bandaged eyes
You'll walk them—not just now, but soon.

—Weldon Kees

After the operation, I lay in the dark for several days, the gauze bandages covering my eyes so completely that only my hands could tell me where I was, what time it was, who was standing before me, a gift of candy or flowers in their sympathetic hands. Three or four times, I woke cockeyed on the bed, my foot at the head, my head at the foot, amazed when the nurse straightened me out at eight o'clock in the morning (according to her).

I spent the days deliciously reminiscing over the calm, white flower of my body twisting mysteriously beneath the sheets in time with some other clock. Blind to propriety—blind!—the necklines of my gowns and pajamas fell down to expose my chest to anyone who happened by. And it was only the snickers of the cafeteria boys or the shocked gasps of the candy stripers that set me patting myself like someone searching for cigarettes or money in a breast pocket.

Through it all there were voices, a voice, that I supposed only I heard (though I found out later that others were tuned in), a voice that spoke in my head like a shortwave radio, an emergency message. A voice from a distant land conjuring the strange condiments and utensils of another cuisine glowing softly under the hood lamp of the General Electric range. I can't remember now if the language was foreign or one of my own. Only something soothing and familiar in the cadences, only the peculiar address to me, kept me listening.

The morning the doctor came to cut off the bandages, I was unexcited, expected a return of the usual, with perhaps a certain rush of vivid sensation. The cold scissors clicked along my cheekbone, I could feel the stubs of my eyelashes, cut down for the operation, coming back to life, fluttering weakly on the doctor's pinkish, flower-smelling hand.

It was awhile before I could actually see anything. The drops

29

they splashed in my eyes took more than a few minutes to work. But then there was the same hospital room I had walked into two weeks before, the same Van Gogh reproduction over the bed, its plastic frame bolted to the wall, the same smiling, doltish Doctor Bowling, who was about to receive $5,276 of my money for restoring my sight. I looked out the window: The world staggered along on its knees in the broken glass of the roadways as it always had, and I waited for the old sick feeling. But for the first time, I could open my eyes and take it all, the strange voice from the all-night world nattering at me somewhere behind my orbitals, telling me not to get sick, telling me to hold my nose, put out my hand and save something.

WHAT WILL HAPPEN

This is the last year for the black walnut tree
in the south field beyond the wooden fence.
The farmer guesses it's seventy or even
eighty years old and doesn't understand
why it's dying.

Next year, no leaves at all, he says.
No walnuts, and the vast, immediate infestation
of insects and fungus
that will eat its way
out from the heart,
until the trunk is just a hull,
toppling lightly into the meadow.

This will happen, we believe, as soon as two or three years from
   now.

Some summer morning, only a few seasons away,
I will walk out drinking coffee
from a purple, hand-thrown mug I used to love,
thinking all is as usual,
and—unaware—become part
of the vast shudder of life deserting the walnut tree,
done with it!
Part of a million lives
springing back to the earth
even though the earth
is no longer a place to hide
or begin again.

But we will leap anyway,
irrelevant things passing before our eyes:
the reddish mole on the face of the star football player
in Trotterville, Tennessee;

the broken wringer of an early-model washing machine,
buried and unidentifiable under rubbish in a garbage dump;
a live rat in the last car of the Lexington Local
in New York City, December 1978;
the various natural and unnatural deaths everyone witnessed
but ignored, or looked away from,
or tried to forget.

And this will all happen very fast
as in the speeded-up motion
of the botanist's camera
recording a cycle of growth or death,
everything forced to an early ending
by the bomb clouds lapping the horizon
that somebody wanted to happen,
and made happen,
and it did.

FOR MIKLOS RADNÓTI: 1909-1944

1.

When Radnóti wrote his last poem for his wife
he was weeks away from death.
He must have known it.
The landscape shook green and terrible
through the long retreat. The guards
pushed Radnóti and the other prisoners
harder, fed them less, whipped them more
often, killed more frequently, with less thought,
the fear of their own death and defeat
making it easier to pull the trigger.

In the midst of the six-month death march,
pissing blood, hair and teeth falling out,
Radnóti kept writing his way out of the nightmare,
tiny poems on postcards and matchbooks.
On the road to Budapest, the guards tortured
a retarded Hungarian boy before they shot him in the mouth.
It was the same in the poems: the prisoners died there, too,
blood running from the ear of Radnóti's friend, the violinist,
the body abandoned in a drainage ditch.

At the end, in the common grave
scrambled up with the human bodies he loved so well,
his poems went down with him,
fierce scraps of life in his coat pockets
that refused to be beaten.
Two years later, the poet gone back
to the earth, the poems remained,
exhumed and reborn,
when the widow plucked them from the fresh, young skeleton.

2.

In Harlem, housing projects shove their way up
out of the earth, all concrete and bricks,
iron bars at the windows, children locked inside
by themselves all day
while the mothers work and the fathers never come back.

I don't know how many people here
read poetry, or love it,
or know the name of Miklos Radnóti,
Hungarian poet dead forty years,
his one book out of print.
I know people love words and music,
listen to radios in the street,
jazz bands in the park,
memorize long passages of soul rap like poetry.
I know Radnóti would have loved my neighbors
who sit all night in Riverside Park
during the long weeks of the heatwave
singing and dancing in the breathless air.

From my window, I see a man on Broadway
propped against a concrete wall.
A brown joint dangles from his mouth
as traffic rushes by obscuring him.
I remember the only photograph I've seen of Radnóti,
a homemade cigarette poked between his Jewish lips,
his wide sexual mouth breathing
the putrid air of World War Two.

When I close the book
the poems still sob around me.
When I turn off the light

the pages remain lit
like the blanched white slats
of a skeleton abandoned
in the war-torn night.
And across the street in Harlem:
the lights flickering off and
off, a chorus of frightened breathing,
a million human hearts
beating steadily in the darkness.

Note

Miklos Radnóti's death occurred as a result of Hungary's wartime alignment
with the Axis powers. During his short life, he was interned several times in
forced-labor camps established by the Hungarian government because of his
political activities (participation in antiwar protests and debates) and his
writing (an early volume was tried for "incitement to rebellion"). It was dur-
ing the last internment, from May to November 1944, that he was executed,
either shot or clubbed to death, and buried in a mass grave near Abda. The
body was exhumed and the last poems retrieved in 1946. The best English
translation of his work, *Clouded Sky* (New York: Harper & Row, 1972),
translated by Polgar, Berg, and Marks, is out of print.

35

CHRISTMAS PARTY

It is my first Scotch I am tinkling
in the crystal glass as I talk to Léonel
in front of the fireplace. Fragrant and fresh
greens bloom along the mantle, hidden lights
blinking among the dark, sleek needles of pine and fir.
Around us, women twirl in long dresses and gloves,
men in tuxedos, someone in a green, glisteny
turban, someone else in high gold heels
that click in lovely, drunken pirouettes
to the flute and cello playing
Vivaldi in the dining room.

Léonel is the only one not drinking. He is explaining
the war, and watching his fiancée, tiny and dark,
the most beautiful woman at the party. Beside her,
the rest of us look like fading moths, a dying breed.
Embarrassed at the tennis shoes she wears
among our delicate pumps and hand-embroidered slippers,
she sits on the sofa hiding her feet,
fingering an uneaten Christmas cookie,
and explaining she does not speak English well
though she understands.

It is all so far away, what Léonel says to me:
the shortage of bread, the way the wounded
bleed lonely in the jungle after the army passes through.
Perhaps Léonel does not want to speak of it
but I ask him anyway what is happening in his country,
ask him why he had to leave, ask him
if his family's in danger, exactly where they live,
persist in knowing precisely
what happened when the farm blew up.

36

Here, as Léonel speaks in his calm, sore voice,
I feel my hand holding my glass of Scotch,
the tiny scratch of ice against the sides,
hear wood burning and falling through the grate,
smell the sweetish smell of applewood, the ghost of fruit.
Next to me, a hand with rings reaches
into a silver bowl of tangerines and walnuts
and comes out full. The luxurious wool
of my trousers bothers me. I feel part
of a long chain of something rich and useless.
I lean forward to catch another word from Léonel. I touch
his arm. I force myself.

GRANDMOTHER, I'M READING TOLSTOY

In the long nights up north,
I've been reading Tolstoy and marveling
at how he knew what everyone
was thinking and even how they felt.
So many people inside him!
A whole city growing and sleeping
and being born. He was a kind master,
knowing exactly what everyone wanted
and loving them for it, no matter what.

I can't begin to imagine how you feel.

In the world I live in it's hard enough
to know *I* hurt when a man on the street
strokes my thigh with his long finger,
or that I marvel at the one-legged woman
hopping and pushing her bike through the park.

You've become something like a golden haystack
so big I couldn't gather it in my arms
if I tried.

I suppose I would like to know
you think it was worth it.

The sunsets up here are unusually painful
this time of year
as if someone raked his fingernails
through a delicate membrane.
I am reading Tolstoy and trying
to understand why you would want to die.
It's a world. All we can do is live
in it. I don't know. It's hard
to share your perspective.
You're at the end of the book.
I haven't gotten very far.
For me, it's still an accomplishment
just to turn over a page.

38

APOLOGIA

If only I could get this song
out of my head I could write
about hurting my husband.
He's just a man with a few hairs
on his head. He has to lie down
on our bed when I hurt him, his eyes
blue zeroes of pain.

The blanket pulled up to his chin,
he looks like the little boy
he used to be: afraid of the dark,
tantalized by fear that kept him
singing sad songs all night long
so he wouldn't break. Lying there,
the fear so strong it was like a disease,
he remembered very little: a blue hairbrush
striking him all the way home from church,
the metal wings on his father's hat,
the summer his mother cried for months.

But I have problems, too:
It is hard for me to share.
I see the top of his head
where his hair is going away
and even that won't stop me
from torturing him. I'm that terrible child
who knows the soft spot in the baby's skull
but puts her finger there anyway,
searching for bone and the place that hurts.

RUSHING AWAY

Sometimes I go to bed at night
hoping I'll wake up happy again.
Remembering Hardy's lines, *as at first
when you were all to me.*

And once in awhile when I awake
in the gold bedroom, in the white bed with brass knobs,
when sun is pressing through the giant boxwood
outside the open window and three cardinals
perch on the cylindrical feeder in the maple tree,
when the air that flows in the window and moves
the white curtain is gentle and likes me,
when you are silent and still sleeping,
twisted and covered in the sheets and comforter,
then I can pretend you are anything I want,
that we are happy again.

Sometimes I can make that feeling last
through the brewing of coffee, grinding
the shiny beans by hand and pouring
the hot water through and smelling it
and watching it drip. I can sit on the front porch
drinking coffee in the rocker and concentrate
on the creak of wood on wood and pretend
our unhappiness never happened.

Then I hear you stirring in the sheets,
your noises in the bathroom, and feel the dread
your tread through the house fills me with.
Something is rising up on terrified, transparent wings
and rushing away, leaving the landscape soundless and gray
till I feel so heavy
as I sit there rocking, torturing the wood.

GEESE IN SNOW

When I clap my hands
even this quietly,
in gloves, in snow,
the geese rise up in darkly broken
circles on the winter sky.
Another perfect form.

In the snow before me
the symmetrical pattern
their wings made, rising
furiously. Far off,
their quiet funnel of sound
settling on the frozen lake.

There is a place for everything,
I think, even I, wild and confused
in the fallen snow.
When I look back to the house
the urge to break the geese
again comes upon me.
In the late afternoon light
one lamp burns through the bubbled glass
of an upstairs window like a captured sun.
My husband is inside, reading.
He wets his thumb methodically.
He turns the pages, one by one.

WHY WE WON'T

have a child
is a continual

source of amazement
to the family

but I have not yet
been able

to reach my arms
around myself

and you are still
holding the shell

to your ear
and wondering

where that empty sound
comes from

ELEGY

Not to be born is the best for man.
—W. H. Auden

I'm sorry: I don't
think much about you anymore.
The child I'm trying to have
takes up all my time these days.
Your old bedroom has been painted
blue and stars pasted on the ceiling.
At night, waking from a dream
a child could believe it's the real thing.

I never let you mean much to me
anyway because I was afraid of you.
Your tiny kicks inside, the unannounced
way you came to me. Those walks we took
were only my way of calming down.
And the field outside town
where I lay down and made you?
It's gone now, grown into a shopping mall.

I've never been able to write you
even one decent letter.
You think I don't care.
There were workmen eating sandwiches
on a brick wall the day you died.
Together, we stepped through the thick red dust.
Remember that song I used to sing you?
Tell me: I don't.

NOT SINGING

for Thomas and Andrew

God stopped and the car
kept rolling backward
over the baby's leg.

And then god started again
because it didn't hurt. He lay there
conscious and uncrying. Cinders
mixed in his yellow hair. Tread marks
red on his broken thigh.

When we got to the hospital
I saw that god had stopped
permanently and was never coming back
to visit these children: the two-year-old
burned everywhere but her face
by her teenage mother. The boy hung
by the neck for wetting the bed.
The little girl with her hands cut off.
An entire hall of bald ones succumbing
to uncured cancers.

When we got to the hospital
I saw the calm, methodical walking
of mothers who knew the truth
and how many days and what the odds
had been from the very beginning.
They were walking constantly through the halls,
sick children slumped in their arms
pushing portable I.V.'s, their hairdos flat,
clothes crumpled and spit up on.
I heard the low telling of favorite stories,
the thousand soothing sounds
that only mothers can make. And then,
in the rare moments when sick children sleep,
the terse trading of hospital stories—

the tracing back of stupid incident
and cruel accident that led them here.
The fathers in their suits or uniforms
coming in after work, standing nervously
beside the tall, white beds and twisting
their caps in their hands or wanting a smoke,
terrified of the supine children
with the far-off look of drugs in their eyes.

Do you know the sound of children
crying in a hospital at night?
You know the smell of a hospital,
and the mechanical, repetitive sounds
of elevators and cardiographs and intravenous pumps.
You remember the hushed voices of visitors,
the uncomfortable feeling of your own good health,
the soundless swoosh of the nurses' shoes,
the drop of air forced from the syringe
before the injection is begun.
But the sound of children crying
in a hospital ward at night? The lights
are turned off early, blinds twirled shut,
toys and crumbs cleared from the sheets.
The children are given their sleeping pills
in sweetened water like soda pop, and the parents
who can stay—those who can leave their other children
home, or those whose child will probably die tonight—
settle on the narrow cots and cannot sleep.

First, there is the steady thump and buzz
of the hospital like a private city that never stops.
Then the whole story of sick children that must be
remembered in spite of oneself.
Every time a little one screamed
and could not be made to feel any better.

45

All the questions that have no answers.
There is the falsely calm breathing
of tranquilized children,
the terrifying rhythm of all of this.
But medications wear off and pain rises again.
The moon rises, the night gets deeper, the city
quieter and even more indifferent, and the sobbing
of children starts filling the air, inarticulate and immediate.
The nurses listen at the door for this to start
and come in with their tiny flashlights
and ask, *are you in pain* and *where does it hurt?*
The children ask for the soda pop
that makes them go to sleep, something to stop
the ruined thigh from jumping out of its tractioned sling
and unsettling the muscles all over again.
For the parents on the cots, there is nothing to do
but lie there and listen and wait for the next drug
and curse god and feel themselves ripping apart inside
and not coming back together in all the same places.

There is so much misery in the world
it cannot be imagined. This is only
one ward of one hospital in one small city.
Beyond this, there's all the other hospitals
and the untamed places where there are no hospitals
but the same diseases, identical pain. There's war and famine,
all the cruelties and violence we inflict on one another,
all the abstractions we keep unspecific.

Now I want to think of happiness
and love and the cured children who live
and go home. The teddy bear in the wheelchair
and the smiles and tight wrinkles
around the eyes of the tired relatives whose child
is wheeled out of brain surgery alive,
their awkward fingers fluttering helplessly
above the green skull cap.
Instead, I think only how odd it is
that people suffer so much, and always have.
Even in my mostly untouched life, I know the breaking
walls of pain inside, and can never imagine
how those with real tragedies go on.
How strong they must be. How strong
and marvelous everyone must be
to bear so much. I'll never understand
how we endure it all or why this is the only gift
we give back to god: how much it hurt,
how much we stood up straight and took.

Shirley Kaufman, *Gold Country*
Etheridge Knight, *The Essential Etheridge Knight*
Ted Kooser, *One World at a Time*
Ted Kooser, *Sure Signs: New and Selected Poems*
Larry Levis, *Winter Stars*
Larry Levis, *Wrecking Crew*
Robert Louthan, *Living in Code*
Tom Lowenstein, tr., *Eskimo Poems from Canada and Greenland*
Archibald MacLeish, *The Great American Fourth of July Parade*
Peter Meinke, *Trying to Surprise God*
Judith Minty, *In the Presence of Mothers*
Carol Muske, *Camouflage*
Carol Muske, *Wyndmere*
Leonard Nathan, *Carrying On: New & Selected Poems*
Leonard Nathan, *Dear Blood*
Leonard Nathan, *Holding Patterns*
Kathleen Norris, *The Middle of the World*
Sharon Olds, *Satan Says*
Alicia Ostriker, *The Imaginary Lover*
Greg Pape, *Black Branches*
Greg Pape, *Border Crossings*
James Reiss, *Express*
Ed Roberson, *Etai-Eken*
William Pitt Root, *Faultdancing*
Liz Rosenberg, *The Fire Music*
Eugene Ruggles, *The Lifeguard in the Snow*
Dennis Scott, *Uncle Time*
Herbert Scott, *Groceries*
Richard Shelton, *Of All the Dirty Words*
Richard Shelton, *Selected Poems, 1969-1981*
Richard Shelton, *You Can't Have Everything*
Arthur Smith, *Elegy on Independence Day*
Gary Soto, *Black Hair*
Gary Soto, *The Elements of San Joaquin*
Gary Soto, *The Tale of Sunlight*
Gary Soto, *Where Sparrows Work Hard*
Tomas Tranströmer, *Windows & Stones: Selected Poems*
Chase Twichell, *Northern Spy*
Chase Twichell, *The Odds*
Constance Urdang, *The Lone Woman and Others*
Constance Urdang, *Only the World*
Ronald Wallace, *Tunes for Bears to Dance To*
Cary Waterman, *The Salamander Migration and Other Poems*
Bruce Weigl, *A Romance*
David P. Young, *The Names of a Hare in English*
Paul Zimmer, *Family Reunion: Selected and New Poems*